Grade 3
Map Skills

Meeting Map Skill Standards with Exploratory Experiences

Written and Edited by
Alaska Hults

Illustrators: Mapping Specialists and Jenny Campbell
Cover Illustrator: Rick Grayson
Designer: Barbara Peterson
Cover Designer: Barbara Peterson
Art Director: Tom Cochrane
Project Director: Carolea Williams

Table of Contents

Introduction

The wonderful thing about teaching children map skills is that they really want to know how to read maps. To children, maps are secret codes that any respectable spy must be able to figure out. Maps are keys to unknown places. Maps hold the promise of an adventure.

The learning standards at the third-grade level are typically very simple. Third graders must

- understand that maps are representational.

- identify geographical features on a map.

- identify, locate, and use the map title, map key, compass rose, lines and borders, roads and routes, and objects and symbols.

- use grid systems to locate communities.

Use the maps and activity pages in *Map Skills: Grade 3* to make your lessons fun and exploratory. Give children the maps, and read aloud the introductory text on the activity page. Have children discuss how the information relates to that map. Discuss with children the questions on the page, and have them work together to solve each problem or follow the directions asked of them.

The maps in this book progress from quite simple to more complex. Use them in order. Full lessons on each map skill are not provided. Supplement difficult concepts with lessons from your social studies curriculum. Schedule about 20 minutes for each map experience. Invite children to bring in maps they find, and have the class examine them. Have the class find the title, key, scale, compass rose, and grid on the map.

Always invite the class to imagine what they could do with each map. The magic in a map is the possibility of new adventures. The skills they use will one day take them safely to the places they want to go. Conveniently, these skills will also transfer well to a standardized-testing situation.

How to Use This Book

Hitting the Map Standards

Before you have children read and complete the activity page that precedes each map, lay a firm foundation for the activity by having children complete the Evaluate the Map reproducible (page 5). This reproducible will keep children's map skills sharp for test-taking and will better prepare them to think critically as they complete the activity page that accompanies the map. Copy the map on an overhead transparency, and display the map so you can point to specific elements of the map during discussion. You may want to use the tips that follow as you do so.

1. Have children work in pairs the first time they complete the reproducible. More details are identified when two pairs of eyes examine the same map.

2. Read the directions to the class. Have children take a moment to look at the map. If there are labels, invite volunteers to read them. Point to each label as it is read, and have the rest of the class follow along. Be sure children understand what each label means before moving on. For example, when children look at the first map, you may explain that when a pond freezes over, often one part will be reserved for free skating and another for games.

3. Children may simply copy the title for question 1. For question 2 they should not repeat the information in the title. Have them carefully examine the map, and say *This map was created by a person. What was the person trying to show or teach in this map?* Record responses on the board.

4. Children may need a thorough review of the map terms before they can complete question 3. Assign colors to each check box, and have children circle or underline parts of the map that correspond to each check box. Invite volunteers to do so on the overhead map.

5. Have children discuss their answers to question 4. Record their responses as a list on the board. When the discussion is complete, point to each word or phrase in the list and read it aloud. Then, encourage children to use the list to write a sentence that answers question 4.

6. For question 5 invite children to simply jot down a keyword or words related to a part of the map that is confusing for them. Collect the reproducibles. Without reading names, quickly go through the reproducibles and read aloud the concerns. Use this information to clarify any areas of the map that are problematic for the class. You may spend more time on this step than on the others, but in return, children are likely to be much more independent as they complete the activity page that accompanies the map.

Name_____ **Date**_____

Evaluate the Map

Use the map to answer the questions.

1. The title is _____.

2. This map shows _____.

3. Check the box. This map has . . .

    ❏ land and water.   ❏ a compass rose.

    ❏ a key.   ❏ grid lines.

    ❏ a scale.   ❏ latitude and/or longitude.

4. How could you use this map?

_____

_____

5. What does not make sense to you?

_____

_____

_____

Map Skills: Grade 3 © 2005 Creative Teaching Press

Using the Activity Pages

Copy the map on an overhead transparency. Decide whether you are going to have children record their responses on the activity page or complete it orally. If you have children do their own work on the activity page, copy it and distribute one to each child. Display the map transparency. Give children time to review the features of the map, and then read aloud the instructional text. Discuss and clarify any new terms. Look over the map, and discuss any confusing symbols or features of the map. Then, walk children through answering the questions or following the direction. Have children respond verbally or record their responses on the activity page. Encourage frequent discussions as you work.

Special Notes

The first few maps all focus on two concepts only: that maps are shown from a bird's-eye-view and that each item on a map represents a real thing. For children who have strong spatial skills, the concept of bird's-eye-view needs almost no explanation. However, many children at this age still struggle with the concept. Try this quick activity to help them understand the concept. In advance, draw a few "blocks" on a large piece of construction paper. Use Monopoly® houses to assemble a simple "town." Have children pretend to be a bird and "fly" slowly over the town. Then, have them return to their seats and draw what they saw. Children may fly over the town more than once to recall all the items.

Pages 10, 20, and 34: Some children may find the maps that go with these activity pages a little busy. Provide children with additional time before the lesson to color in the map. As children color in each element of the map, they will focus on the meaning and location of symbols and key map features and be better prepared to read the map.

Page 22: Give each child two 7/8" squares. Have children line up the edges of a square with the scale line to confirm that the length of the square equals 400 ft. Have them use the square to measure distances. Show children how to place the corner of the square on their starting location and mark the ending location on the edge of the square when they want to compare distances. Have them place the two squares side-by-side to measure longer distances. Some distances on this activity page do not require the use of the scale. Children should be able to determine more than and less than just by estimating the distances.

Pages 32 and 34: The maps that go with these activity pages aim to expose children to the use of latitude and longitude. You can begin by having children observe and discuss the lines on a globe. children should notice that the lines go all the way around the globe, that lines of longitude are far apart at the equator and come closer and closer together until they cross at the poles, and they should be reminded often that the lines are imaginary. Later, have children compare the maps with lines of latitude and longitude and those with a grid. Make sure they are clear that the two systems work differently. Finally, invite children who are curious about the lines to research special lines such as the prime meridian, the Tropic lines, and the Arctic Circle and Antarctic Circle.

Build a map center. Laminate each map. You may want to make two copies and put the answer key on the back of each map. Place the maps at the center with wipe-off markers and erasers. Provide additional atlases and at least one globe for children to examine.

- Have children compare the maps to each other. Do they all have titles? Do they all show the scale? How many of the maps have a grid? How are some of the symbols alike and different? What kinds of maps are easiest for them to read? Invite children to record their thoughts by jotting down key words in a map journal.

- Provide examples of simple and ornate compass roses. Provide long, thin paper triangles, glue, decorative items such as sequins, feathers, and glitter, and a large piece of construction paper. Invite children to make their own compass rose. Have children label each direction on the compass.

- Provide die-cuts and large sheets of butcher paper. Invite children to make maps (suggest pirate maps, treasure maps, or maps that show how they get from home to school) using the die-cuts as symbols.

- Cover a large bulletin board with a 5-by-5 grid using yarn. Label the grid with index cards so that each column is numbered and each row is lettered. Place an index card labeled with a student name in each box. Obtain or create two large dice. Write a letter or number that matches the grid on each side of the dice. For calling on volunteers, lining up to go to recess or lunch, or for choosing classroom responsibilities, roll each die and match the letter and number that turn faceup to a name in the grid.

- Add grids to the maps that do not have them, and ask children to find certain items using the grid.

- Give each child a copy of three maps. Play "I Spy" with the class, having them locate the compass rose, the title, the scale, and small details in each map.

- Have children choose a favorite map. Have them come up with three quiz questions for that map, write each question on a slip of paper, and place the papers in a jar. At the end of the day, pull two questions from the jar and have children determine which map contains the answer to the question. Then, have children find the answer to the question.

Hockey Puck Park
Maps Show Places

Read.

Maps are pictures that show where things are. You could draw a map of your desk. You could draw a map of your house. You could draw a map of your town.

You read a map to get information. This map shows a neighborhood park. If you needed to go to somewhere in the park, you could use the map to figure out how to get there.

Use the map to answer the questions. Follow the directions.
You will need crayons for this activity.

1. Look at the map. What would you most like to do in Hockey Puck Park?

   _____

2. How many ponds are shown on the map? _____

3. If you walked in a straight line from the Native Forest to the Duck Pond, would you cross the path? _____

4. If your father drove you to Hockey Puck Park, could he park the car right beside the Community Center? Why?

   _____

5. Use your yellow crayon to color along Edge Lane.

6. Which 2 streets pass right by the gazebo?

   _____   _____

Map Skills: Grade 3 © 2005 Creative Teaching Press

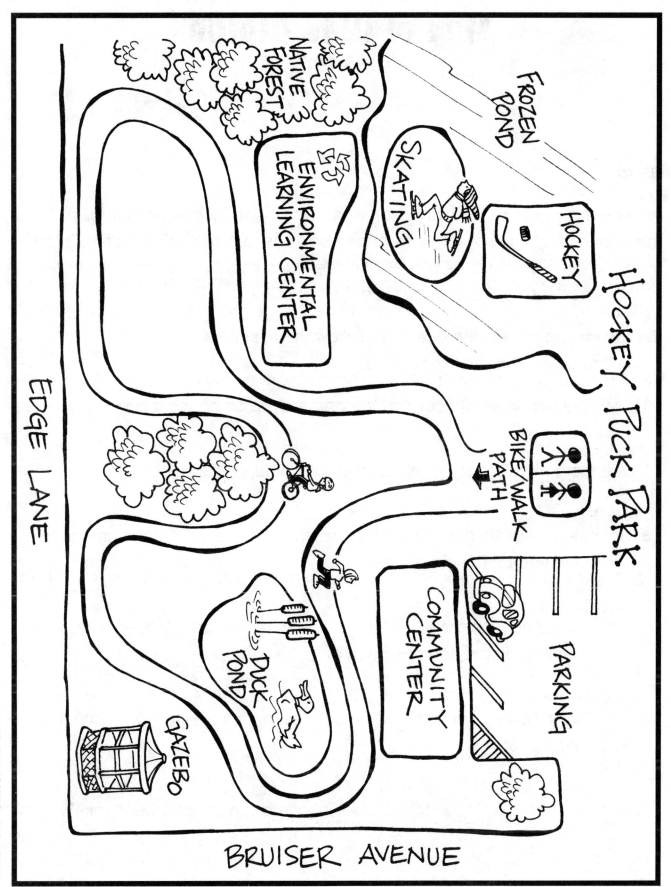

HOCKEY PUCK PARK

FROZEN POND

NATIVE FOREST

ENVIRONMENTAL LEARNING CENTER

SKATING

HOCKEY

BIKE/WALK PATH

EDGE LANE

DUCK POND

COMMUNITY CENTER

PARKING

GAZEBO

BRUISER AVENUE

Name_____ Date_____

Map of Olde Albion
The Key

Read.

The **key** tells what the map symbols mean. A map symbol can be a small picture that shows where one object is. Maps symbols can also give information. On this map, the key shows you fun places (like rides) and important places (like bathrooms). Read the key before you read the rest of the map.

Use the map to answer the questions. Follow the directions.
You will need crayons for this activity.

1. Use your red crayon to color all the games symbols on the map.

2. Are there more places to get food or take a ride in Olde Albion?
   _____

3. Imagine you get hurt inside the Blacksmith Shop. Use your green crayon to circle the nearest first aid station.

4. If you became thirsty while watching a show at the Tudor Stage, could you buy a drink on Robin Hood Highway? _____

5. Use your yellow crayon to draw the quickest path from the Front Gate to the Royal Puppet Stage.

6. Is there a bathroom closer to the Royal Theatre or the Olde Globe Theatre?
   _____

Map Skills: Grade 3 © 2005 Creative Teaching Press

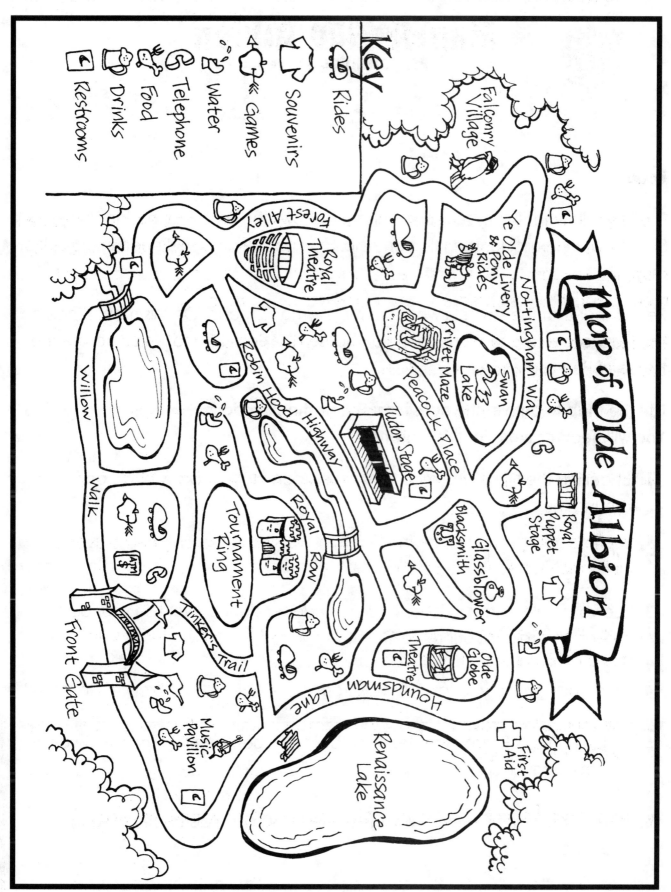

Map Skills: Grade 3 © 2005 Creative Teaching Press

The Capitol
Maps Show Places

Read.

The **title** tells what the map shows. This map shows the area around the United States Capitol building. The title can help you find the map you need in a book of maps.

Remember that the key tells what the map symbols mean. On this map, labels on the Capitol building tell you which side houses the Senate and which houses the House of Representatives.

Use the map to answer the questions. Follow the directions.
You will need crayons for this activity.

1. Underline the title of the map with your green crayon. Draw a red box around the key.

2. Which interstate highway is on the map? _____

3. Use your yellow crayon to color along Independence Ave. Use your blue crayon to circle the Supreme Court.

4. What road would you take to walk from the Senate to the Library of Congress?
   _____

5. Which House of Representatives office building is between the Rayburn Building and the Cannon Building? _____

6. Which two Senate office buildings are within walking distance of the Supreme Court?
   _____

Map Skills: Grade 3 © 2005 Creative Teaching Press

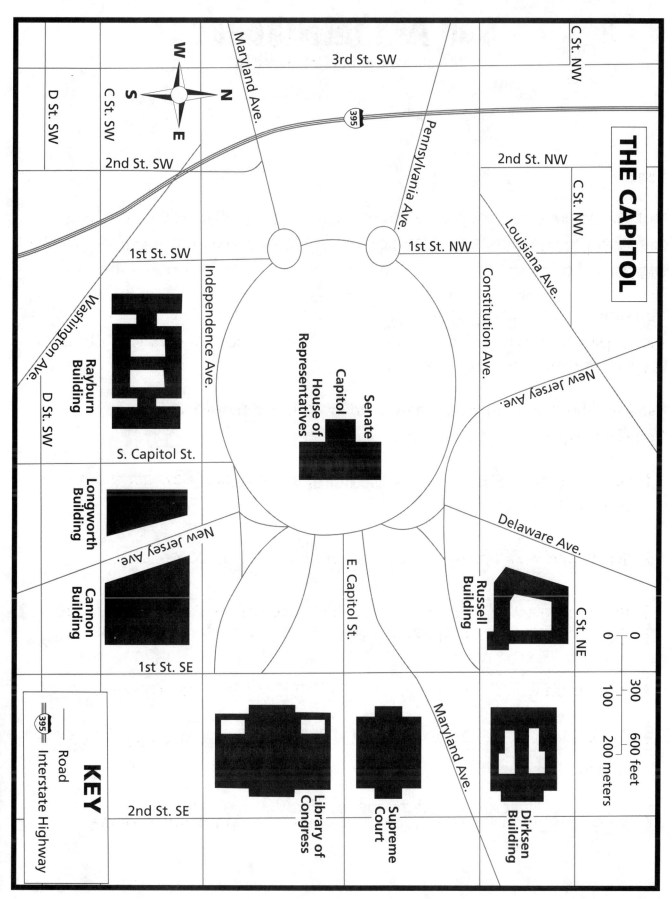

THE CAPITOL

KEY

—— Road

🛣 395 Interstate Highway

Map Skills: Grade 3 © 2005 Creative Teaching Press

San Antonio, Texas
Maps Show Relationships

Read.

Maps show how near or far two places are from each other. They show what direction you would go to get from one place to another. Maps can help you understand a person's path of travel. For example, if you look at this map you can see that the library and post office are next to each other. This map shows a part of the city of San Antonio, Texas.

Use the map to answer the questions.

1. What is the name of the railroad in this part of San Antonio?

   _____

2. Which is closer to the pool: the theater or the courthouse?

   _____

3. Which road would you cross if you walked from the train station to the church?

   _____

4. Would Booker Alley be a good street to take if you were going from the school to the library? Why?

   _____

5. Which building is on 8th St.? _____

6. Use your green crayon to draw the route you would walk from the library to the train station.

Map Skills: Grade 3 © 2005 Creative Teaching Press

SAN ANTONIO, TEXAS

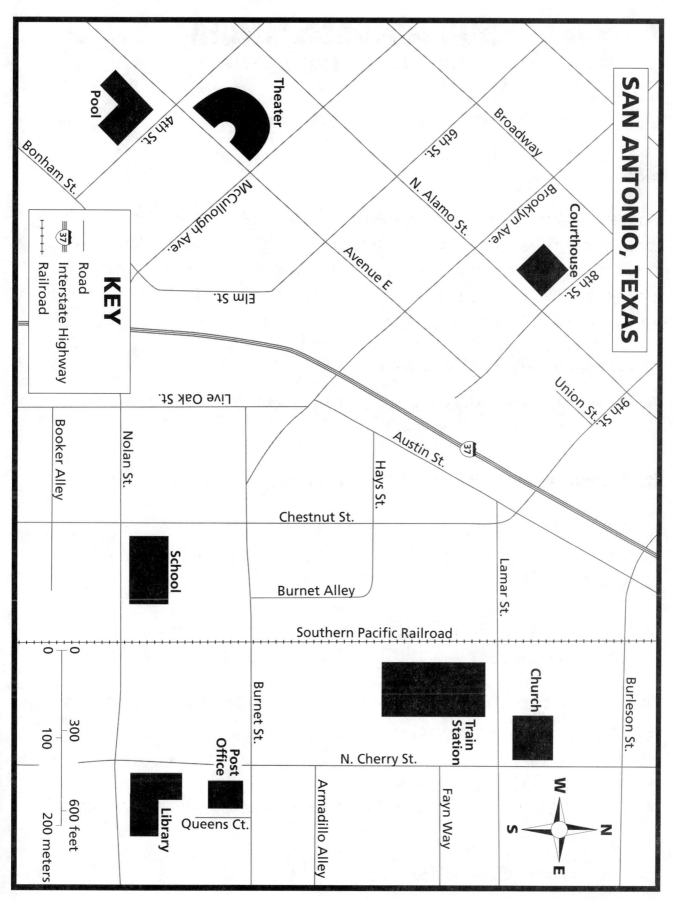

KEY

— Road

🛣 37 Interstate Highway

+++++ Railroad

Pool

Theater

4th St.

Bonham St.

McCullough Ave.

Elm St.

Broadway

6th St.

N. Alamo St.

Brooklyn Ave.

Avenue E

Courthouse

8th St.

9th St.

Union St.

Live Oak St.

Austin St.

37

Hays St.

Chestnut St.

Booker Alley

Nolan St.

School

Burnet Alley

Lamar St.

Southern Pacific Railroad

Burnet St.

Post Office

Queens Ct.

Library

Armadillo Alley

N. Cherry St.

Train Station

Church

Fayn Way

Burleson St.

W N E S

0   0
       300
100
       600 feet
200 meters

The San Juan Islands
Review

Read.

Maps show direction with a **compass rose**. A compass rose tells which way is north on the map.

Simple

N

Detailed

N
W E
S

The **cardinal directions** are north, south, east, and west. The **ordinal** directions are northeast, northwest, southeast, and southwest.

Use the map to answer the questions.

1. Use your purple crayon to circle the compass rose.

2. Which park is farthest west? _____

3. Which island is farthest north? _____

4. If you sailed from Spieden Island to Waldron, which direction would you travel?

    _____

5. If you lived in Richardson, which direction would you have to go to reach San Juan National Historical Park? _____

6. How many towns are on this map? **Hint:** To avoid counting a town twice, cross off each town with a crayon as you count it. _____

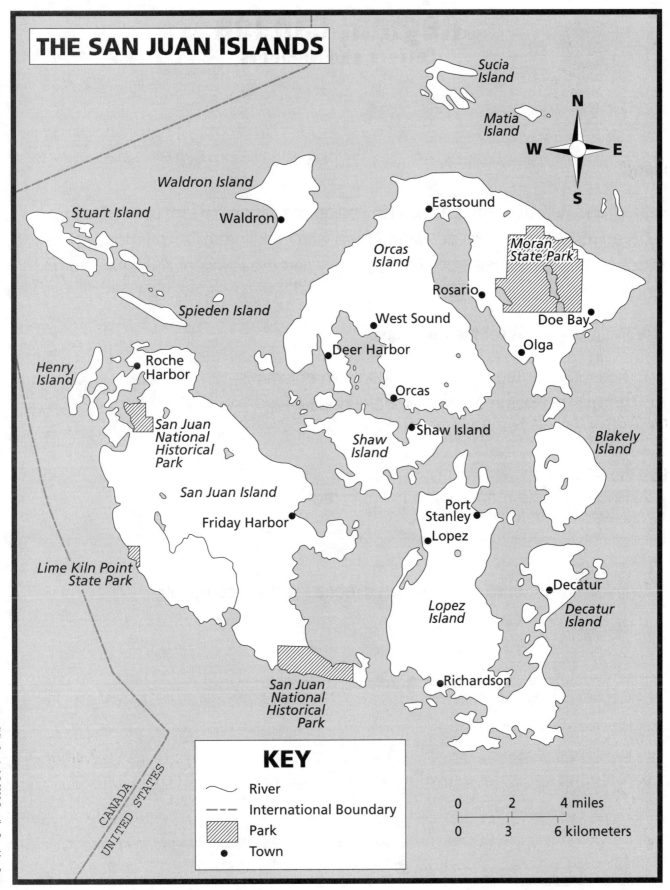

THE SAN JUAN ISLANDS

Sucia Island

Matia Island

N
W   E
S

Waldron Island

● Eastsound

Stuart Island

Waldron ●

Orcas Island

Moran State Park

Rosario ●

Spieden Island

West Sound ●

Doe Bay

● Olga

Henry Island

Roche Harbor ●

Deer Harbor ●

Blakely Island

San Juan National Historical Park

Orcas ●

● Shaw Island

Shaw Island

San Juan Island

Friday Harbor ●

Port Stanley ●

Lime Kiln Point State Park

Lopez ●

Decatur ●

Decatur Island

Lopez Island

San Juan National Historical Park

● Richardson

CANADA

UNITED STATES

KEY

〜 River

--- International Boundary

▨ Park

● Town

0   2   4 miles

0   3   6 kilometers

Name_____ **Date**_____

Regina, Canada
Letters and Numbers

Read.

Letters and numbers can be useful in finding places on a map. Look at the lettered rows. Trace them across the map with your finger. On this map, at the place where row B meets column 4, you will find the towns of Yorktown, Sturgis, and Melville.

Use the map to answer the questions.

1. True or False: The provincial capital is in column 3. _____
   What is the name of the provincial capital? _____

2. Find B2 on the map. List the towns in that section.

   _____ _____ _____ _____

3. If you flew from A1 to A4, which direction would you travel?

   _____

4. Porcupine Provincial Forest is in which column number? _____

5. Write the letter of the row that Trans-Canada Highway 1 travels through.

   _____

6. True or False: There is a lake in column 2. _____

Map Skills: Grade 3 © 2005 Creative Teaching Press

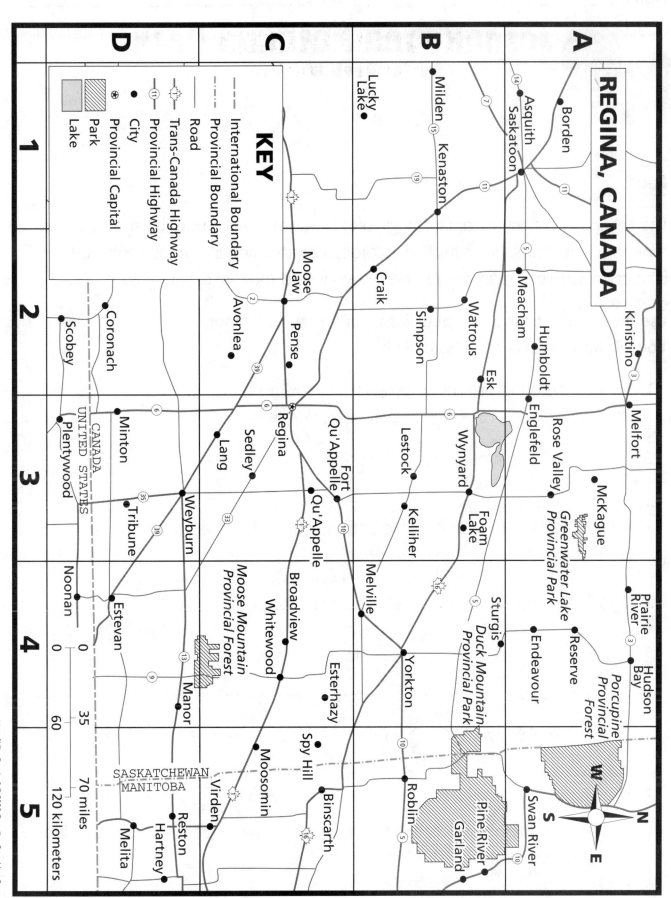

REGINA, CANADA

KEY

- - -	International Boundary
-·-·-	Provincial Boundary
——	Road
✧	Trans-Canada Highway
⑪	Provincial Highway
●	City
⊛	Provincial Capital
▨	Park
▢	Lake

	1	2	3	4	5
A					
B					
C					
D					

Borden
Asquith
Saskatoon
Kinistino
Milden
Kenaston
Meacham
Humboldt
Esk
Englefeld
Rose Valley
Melfort
Prairie River
McKague
Greenwater Lake Provincial Park
Lucky Lake
Craik
Watrous
Simpson
Wynyard
Foam Lake
Sturgis
Duck Mountain Provincial Park
Endeavour
Reserve
Hudson Bay
Porcupine Provincial Forest
Moose Jaw
Avonlea
Pense
Regina
Fort Qu'Appelle
Lestock
Kelliher
Melville
Yorkton
Roblin
Pine River Garland
Swan River
Sedley
Lang
Qu'Appelle
Broadview
Whitewood
Esterhazy
Spy Hill
Moosomin
Binscarth
Minton
Weyburn
Tribune
Plentywood
Noonan
Estevan
Manor
Reston
Hartney
Melita
Virden
Scobey
Coronach

Moose Mountain Provincial Forest

CANADA
UNITED STATES

SASKATCHEWAN
MANITOBA

N W S E

0   0   0
35   60
70 miles
120 kilometers

Map Skills: Grade 3 © 2005 Creative Teaching Press

Regina, Canada 19

Name_____ Date_____

Joshua Tree National Park
Review

Read.

The key gives you important information about the symbols on the map. For example, this maps shows that large groups must camp in a different place than individual families. Read the key before you read the rest of the map.

Use the map to answer the questions. Follow the directions.
You will need crayons for this activity.

1. Is there a site for groups to camp at Sheep Pass? _____

2. Is there a picnic site on Eureka Peak? _____

3. Follow the Utah Trail south. Which campground is closest to the North Entrance Station? _____

4. You are staying in Black Rock Canyon and want to see Hidden Valley. Use your green crayon to draw the route.

5. Your friend twists her ankle on Queen Mountain. Use your red crayon to circle the nearest medical facility.

6. If you were camping at Ryan Mountain, would there be drinking water at the campground? _____

Map Skills: Grade 3 © 2005 Creative Teaching Press

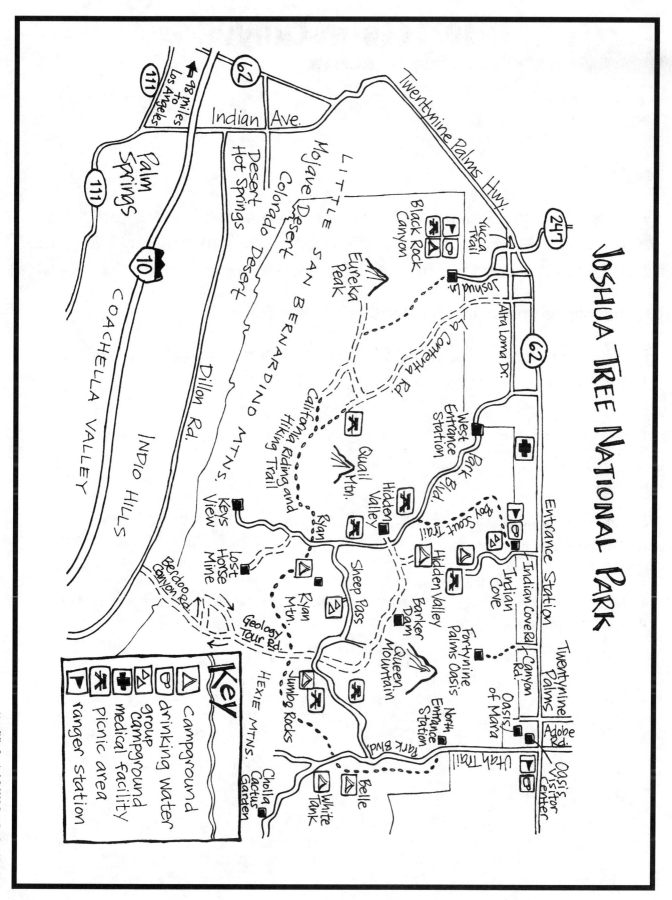

Joshua Tree National Park

Key

- △ campground
- ⊡ drinking water
- △ group campground
- ✚ medical facility
- ✕ picnic area
- ▽ ranger station

Map Skills: Grade 3 © 2005 Creative Teaching Press

Horsethief Canyon
Review

Read.

The scale of the map is a line that tells you what distance is represented by each inch or centimeter. It is usually in a bottom corner. On this map, every 7/8" equals 400 ft. Every 23 mm equals 120 meters.

Use the map to answer the questions.

1. Circle the scale in blue crayon. Is the school longer or shorter than 400 ft (120 m) wide? _____

2. If you wanted to live closer to the pool, where would you buy a house: Eagles Nest Dr. or Gold Rush Dr.? _____

3. What is the approximate length of Roan Circle in inches/millimeters? Is this more or less than 400 ft (120 m)? _____
   _____

4. Find Bunkerhill Dr. Use your red crayon to circle the corner of Bunkerhill Dr. and Deer Creek Ct.

5. Name the grid sections through which Bunkerhill Dr. travels.
   _____ _____ _____

6. Find the corner of Calendula St. and Palomino Creek Dr. Circle it with your green crayon. Then use the crayon to show what roads you would take to get to the school.

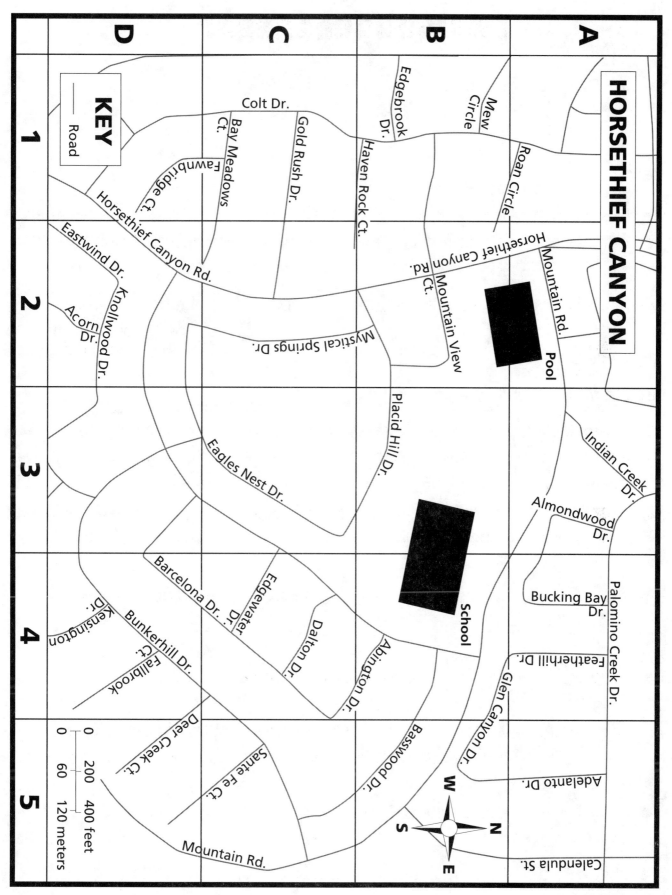

HORSETHIEF CANYON

KEY
— Road

Pool

School

Mew Circle
Roan Circle
Edgebrook Dr.
Haven Rock Ct.
Mountain Rd.
Horsethief Canyon Rd.
Mountain View Ct.
Mystical Springs Dr.
Indian Creek Dr.
Almondwood Dr.
Placid Hill Dr.
Colt Dr.
Gold Rush Dr.
Bay Meadows Ct.
Fawnbridge Ct.
Horsethief Canyon Rd.
Eastwind Dr.
Knollwood Dr.
Acorn Dr.
Eagles Nest Dr.
Barcelona Dr.
Edgewater Dr.
Dalton Dr.
Abington Dr.
Bucking Bay Dr.
Palomino Creek Dr.
Featherhill Dr.
Kensington Dr.
Bunkerhill Dr.
Fallbrook Ct.
Deer Creek Ct.
Sante Fe Ct.
Basswood Dr.
Glen Canyon Dr.
Adelanto Dr.
Calendula St.
Mountain Rd.

0   200   400 feet
0   60   120 meters

N W E S

Name_____ Date_____

Petaluma, CA
Review

Read.

A **grid** is used on many maps to help break up the area into smaller pieces. Then, you can use the pieces to find places. You usually say the letter first and then the number.

Most road maps use a grid and an index to help you find places. An index is a list of important places on the map and the letter and number of the piece of the map where they can be found.

Use the map and index to answer the questions.

Acapulco Ct.	B4	Kresky Ct.	C1	Putnam Way	A3
Alta Dr.	A2	Mark Dr.	C4	Santa Barbara Way	D4
Crinella Dr.	A2-D5	Pool	C5	School	B4

1. What park is found in A1? _____

2. Use your blue crayon to color along U.S. Highway 101. The highway is in which 3 grids?

   _____   _____   _____

3. Use the index above to find Alta Dr. Color along it with a green crayon.

4. Use the index above to find the school. Circle it with your red crayon. List the grid sections that the school is in. _____   _____

5. If you lived on Mark Dr., would you have a shorter walk to the school or the pool?

   _____

6. Use the index above to find Crinella Dr. Color along it in purple.

PETALUMA, CA

KEY

- —— Road
- ==(101)== U.S. Highway
- ▨ Park

Kenilworth Park and Fairgrounds

McDowell Park

Compass: N, S, E, W

Scale: 0 — 400 — 800 feet / 0 — 150 — 300 meters

School

Pool

Tennis Courts

Map Skills: Grade 3 © 2005 Creative Teaching Press

Name_____ Date_____

Pirate Map
Review

Read.

Congratulations! You have just been made First Mate on the pirate ship *Black Scourge*. Your captain wants you to prove that you are trustworthy by double-checking that the treasure map is correct. He tells you that the **scale** of a map is a line that shows how many miles and/or kilometers are represented by each inch. It is usually in the bottom corner.

Use the map to answer Captain Jack's questions.
You will need crayons for this activity.

1. Arg, matey! I've drawn this map so that every 1½ inches equals 5 miles. About how wide is the island at its widest point? _____

2. Find the start of the path at Black Lagoon. Use your green crayon to make an X 5 miles from the start of the path.

3. If a bird flew from Dead Man's Waterfall to Treasure Camp, would it fly 5 miles or 10 miles, matey? _____

4. Which is closer to Treasure Camp: the nearest shore of Blue Lagoon or the nearest shore of Black Lagoon? _____

5. About how far is it between Monster Mountain and the farthest palm tree?
    _____

6. Once I've made it as far as Serpent Pass, about how far do I have left to go before I can dig my hands into the chest of rubies and gold?
    _____

Map Skills: Grade 3 © 2005 Creative Teaching Press

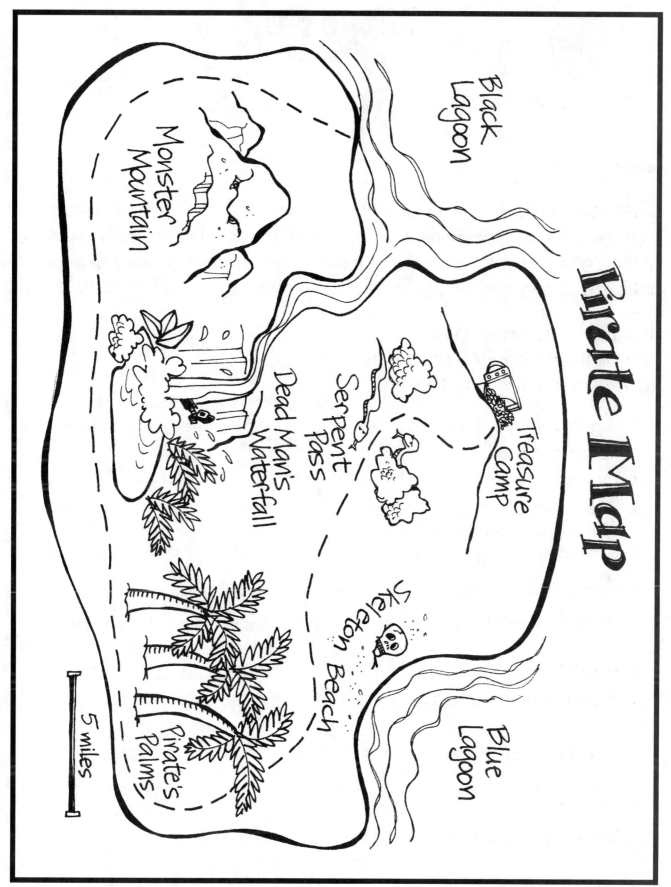

Pirate Map

Black Lagoon

Blue Lagoon

Monster Mountain

Treasure Camp

Dead Man's Waterfall

Serpent Pass

Skeleton Beach

Pirate's Palms

5 miles

Japan 1
Political Maps

Read.

A **political map** is used for learning about the territory and capital city of a country. It shows us the places people have built and the borders between countries. There are five countries on this map. The dashed lines show you the borders in between them and the names of the countries are written in capital letters.

Use the map to answer the questions. Follow the directions.
You will need crayons for this activity.

1. Find the capital city of Japan. Circle it with your yellow crayon. What is its name?

   _____

2. List the 5 countries shown on the map. _____ _____

   _____   _____   _____

3. If you were on a ship sailing from Akita to Russia, which direction would you travel?

   _____

4. Use your orange crayon to draw along the border between China and Russia.

5. On this map, does China have land along the Sea of Japan? _____

6. Color the island of Shikoku green.

Map Skills: Grade 3 © 2005 Creative Teaching Press

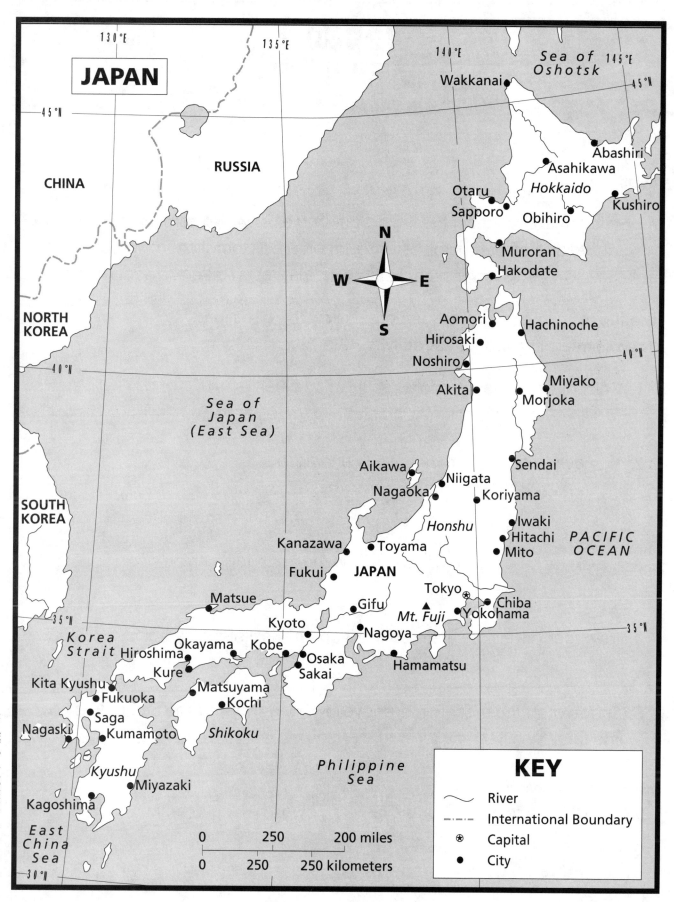

JAPAN

RUSSIA

CHINA

Sea of Oshotsk

Wakkanai

Abashiri

Asahikawa

Otaru
Sapporo

Hokkaido

Kushiro

Obihiro

Muroran
Hakodate

NORTH KOREA

Aomori
Hirosaki

Hachinoche

Noshiro

Miyako

Akita

Morjoka

Sea of Japan (East Sea)

SOUTH KOREA

Sendai

Aikawa
Nagaoka

Niigata

Koriyama

Honshu

Iwaki
Hitachi
Mito

PACIFIC OCEAN

Kanazawa

Toyama

Fukui

JAPAN

Tokyo

Matsue

Gifu

Chiba
Yokohama

Kyoto

Mt. Fuji

Nagoya

Korea Strait

Okayama

Kobe

Hamamatsu

Hiroshima

Osaka

Kure

Sakai

Kita Kyushu

Matsuyama

Fukuoka

Kochi

Saga

Shikoku

Nagaski

Kumamoto

Kyushu

Philippine Sea

Miyazaki

Kagoshima

East China Sea

KEY

〜 River

‑‑‑ International Boundary

⊛ Capital

● City

0   250   200 miles

0   250   250 kilometers

Map Skills: Grade 3 © 2005 Creative Teaching Press

Japan 2
Physical Maps

Read.

A **physical map** can show the landforms, bodies of water, climate, soil, plant and animal life, and other natural resources of an area. Sometimes physical maps use color to show elevation (how high the land is) or even different ecosystems.

Use the map to answer the questions. Follow the directions.
You will need crayons for this activity.

1. Color all of the rivers and lakes on this map blue.

2. Name the bodies of water that surround Japan.

   _____   _____   _____

   _____   _____   _____

3. Do all the mountain ranges in Japan run north to south? _____

4. How many rivers are there on the island of Hokkaido? _____

5. Shade all of the mountain areas yellow. How many of the 5 countries have mountains on this map?   _____

6. A bird flying from Mt. Fuji to Kyushu is going in which direction?

   _____

Map Skills: Grade 3 © 2005 Creative Teaching Press

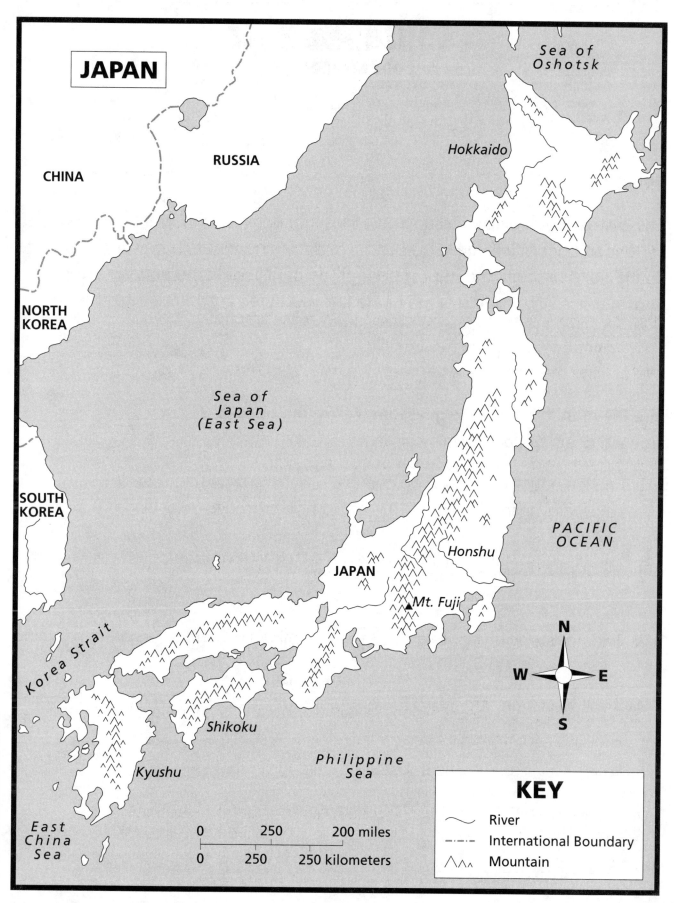

JAPAN

CHINA

RUSSIA

*Sea of
Oshotsk*

Hokkaido

NORTH
KOREA

*Sea of
Japan
(East Sea)*

SOUTH
KOREA

PACIFIC
OCEAN

Honshu

JAPAN

▲*Mt. Fuji*

Korea Strait

N

W   E

S

Shikoku

Kyushu

*Philippine
Sea*

*East
China
Sea*

| 0 | 250 | 200 miles |
| 0 | 250 | 250 kilometers |

KEY

〜   River

–·–·–   International Boundary

∧∧∧   Mountain

Name_____ Date_____

South America
Latitude

Read.

The earth is divided up with imaginary lines that help us find places and measure distances. Lines of **latitude** run around the globe and measure how far places are to the north or south. The most important line of latitude is the **equator**—a line drawn around the middle of the globe. It is measured 0°, and all other lines of latitude are measured north or south of it.

We call the measurements **degrees**. We write degrees using the ° symbol.

Use the map to answer the questions. Follow the directions.
You will need crayons for this activity.

1. Find the equator on your map and use your red crayon to color along it. Use your yellow crayon to color along 10°N and a blue crayon to color along 10°S.

2. What line of latitude passes through Venezuela? _____

3. Find Paraguay on the map. What line of latitude runs through it?

   _____

4. If you went from Argentina to Venezuela, which direction would you travel?

   _____

5. Which countries does the equator pass through in South America?

   _____   _____

6. Chile is a long, thin country. How many lines of latitude pass through it?

   _____

Map Skills: Grade 3 © 2005 Creative Teaching Press

SOUTH AMERICA

90°W   80°W   70°W   60°W   50°W   40°W

Caribbean Sea

10°N   10°N

VENEZUELA

GUYANA

SURINAME

COLOMBIA

FRENCH GUIANA
(FRANCE)

0°   Equator   Equator   0°

ECUADOR

*Galapagos
Islands
(Ecuador)*

Amazon R.

BRAZIL

10°S   10°S

PERU

*PACIFIC
OCEAN*

BOLIVIA

N

W   **E**

S

20°S   20°S

PARAGUAY

30°S   30°S

CHILE

ARGENTINA

URUGUAY

*ATLANTIC
OCEAN*

KEY

〜   River

‒·‒·‒   International Boundary

40°S   40°S

0	500	1000 miles
0	500	1000 kilometers

50°S   50°S

*Falkland Islands
(United Kingdom)*

*South Georgia
(United Kingdom)*

100°S   90°S   80°S   70°S   60°S   50°S   40°S   30°S

Asia
Longitude

Read.

In order to talk about where places are on the earth, scientists invented imaginary lines to divide it into sections. Lines of **longitude** measure how far places are east or west around the earth. They run from the North Pole to the South Pole.

We call the measurements degrees. We write **degrees** using the ° symbol.

Use the map to answer the questions. Follow the directions.
You will need crayons for this activity.

1. Find the compass rose and circle it with your yellow crayon. Then find the North Pole (where all the lines of longitude meet) and color it red.

2. The lines of longitude are labeled across the bottom of your map. Find 90°E and color along it with your blue crayon.

3. True or False: The line for 90°E passes through China. _____

4. Find Yemen on the map. What line of longitude passes through it?

   _____

5. Find the island country of Sri Lanka. What line of longitude passes through it?

   _____

6. Find Georgia on the map. Color along the line of longitude that passes through Georgia with your purple crayon.

Map Skills: Grade 3 © 2005 Creative Teaching Press

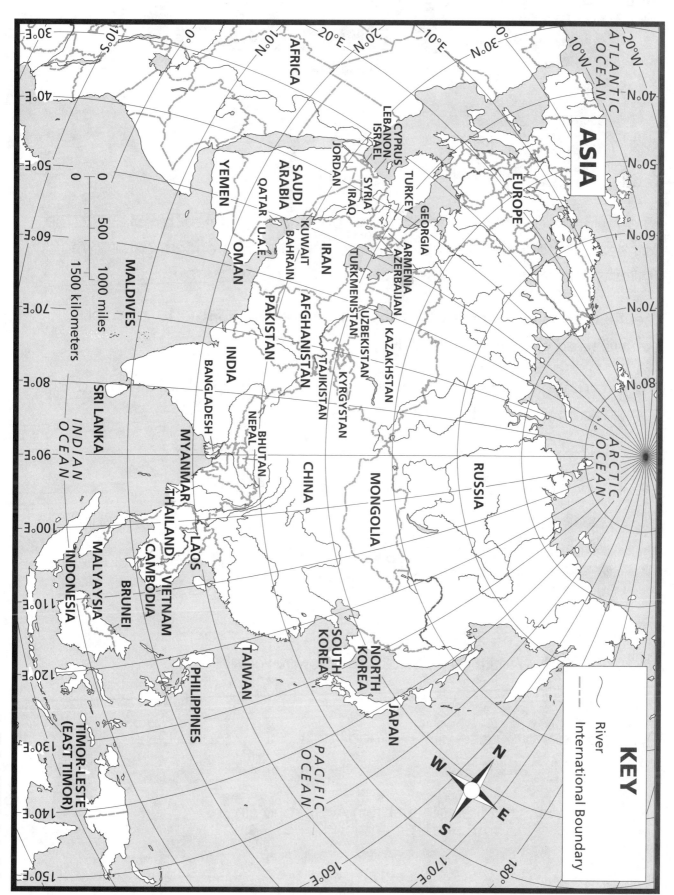

ASIA

KEY

- River
- International Boundary

Map Skills: Grade 3 © 2005 Creative Teaching Press

Fargo, North Dakota
Review

Read.

Fargo is located in an area that used to be an ancient lake, Lake Agassiz. The flatness of the area makes flooding a problem because once the river overflows its banks it spreads great distances.

Use the map to answer the questions. Follow the directions.
You will need crayons for this activity.

1. If you needed to go from Concordia College to Island Park, which 3 roadways would let you cross the river?

    _____ _____ _____

2. In which grid section is the Dakota Heartland Hospital? _____

3. If you lived on Foss St., would Woodlawn Park or Island Park be closer to your home? _____

4. Can you drive south on 10th St. S? How do you know?

    _____

5. Does Highway 10 cross either railroad track? _____

6. Draw a red star at the corner of 10th Ave. S. and 6th St S.

Map Skills: Grade 3 © 2005 Creative Teaching Press

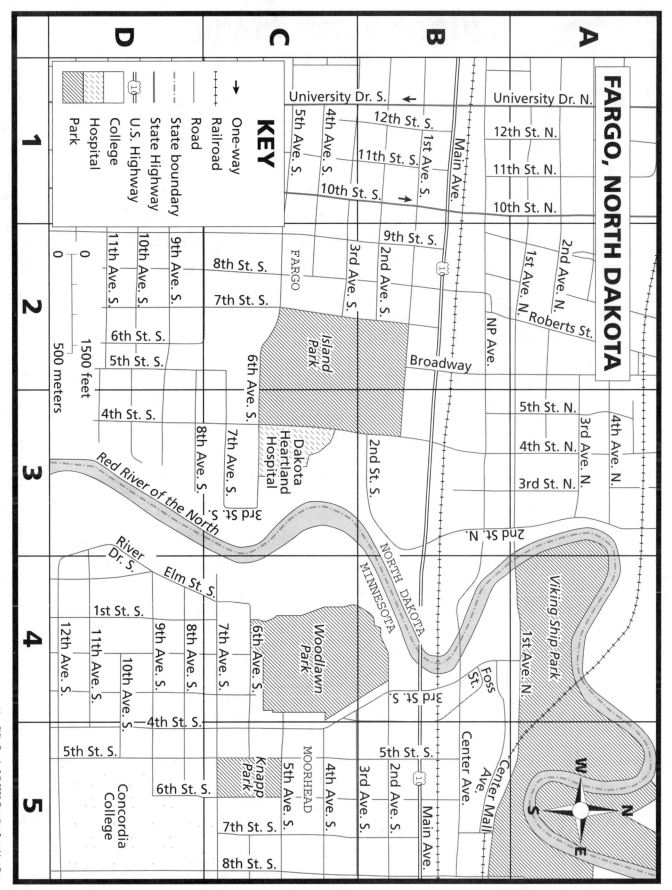

FARGO, NORTH DAKOTA

KEY

→ One-way
┼┼┼ Railroad
Road
State Highway
State boundary
U.S. Highway
College
Hospital
Park

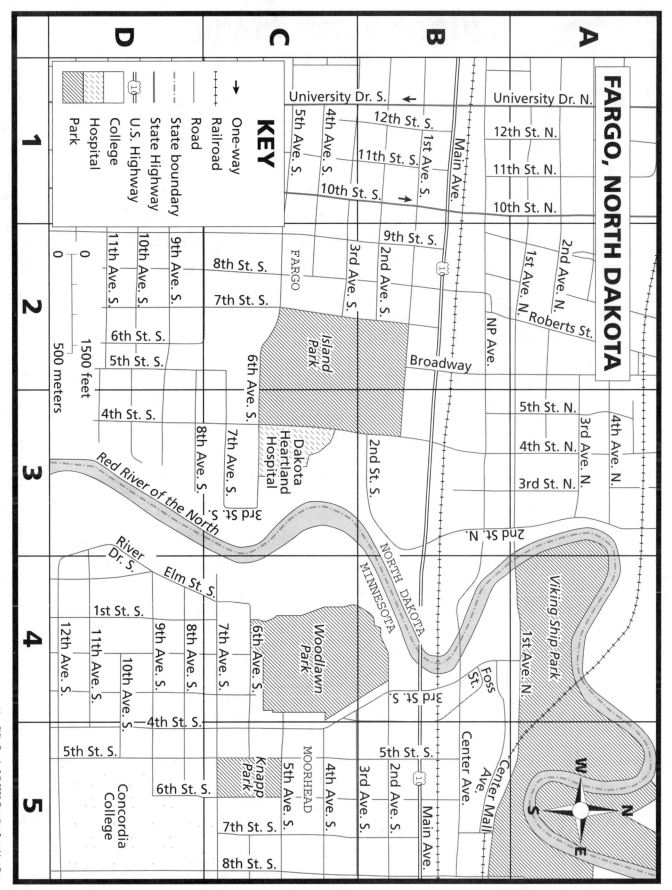

Name_____ Date_____

Idaho Falls, Idaho
Review

Read.

Idaho Falls was a crossroads, a resting place for travelers on their way to other places. Idaho Falls was the location of early bridges that helped traders, trains, and pioneers cross the Snake River on their way to someplace else.

Use the map to answer the questions. Follow the directions.
You will need crayons for this activity.

1. Color the Snake River blue.

2. If you face north, in which direction would you turn to drive to Highway 15?

   _____

3. If you lived on Atlanta St. in B2, what would be the shortest route to Casseopeia St. in A1?

   _____

4. What is the symbol for railroad on this map?

5. Find the error in the index and correct it.

Idaho Ave.	A5-B5	Saturn Cir.	B1-B2
Legion Dr.	B4	S. Pioneer Rd.	D2
Milligan Rd.	D3	Vassar Way	B1

Map Skills: Grade 3 © 2005 Creative Teaching Press

IDAHO FALLS, IDAHO

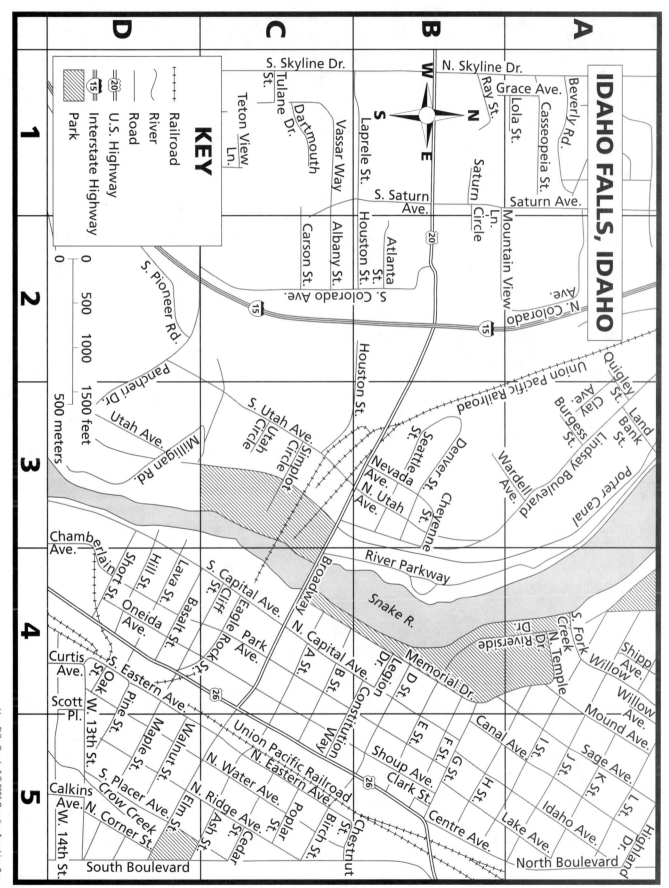

KEY

┼┼┼	Railroad
∿	River
—	Road
20	U.S. Highway
15	Interstate Highway
▨	Park

Map Skills: Grade 3 © 2005 Creative Teaching Press

Nova Scotia
Review

Read.

The funnel shape of the Bay of Fundy creates the highest tides on Earth. The difference between high tide and low tide can be up to 48 ft (14 m)! Twice daily, 200 billion tons of water enter and leave the bay—equal to all the rivers on the planet!

Use the map to answer the questions. Follow the directions.
You will need crayons for this activity.

1. Use your green crayon to draw along the provincial boundary between New Brunswick and Nova Scotia.

2. Color along 66°W with your blue crayon. Does 66°W pass through the Bay of Fundy? _____

3. Could you sail to Bridgewater? _____

4. If you walked from Yarmouth to the other end of Nova Scotia, which direction would you travel? _____

5. Measure Nova Scotia from Yarmouth to the northeastern tip of Cape Breton Island. Roughly how far is it in miles/kilometers? _____

6. Which city is farthest south on the map? _____

Map Skills: Grade 3 © 2005 Creative Teaching Press

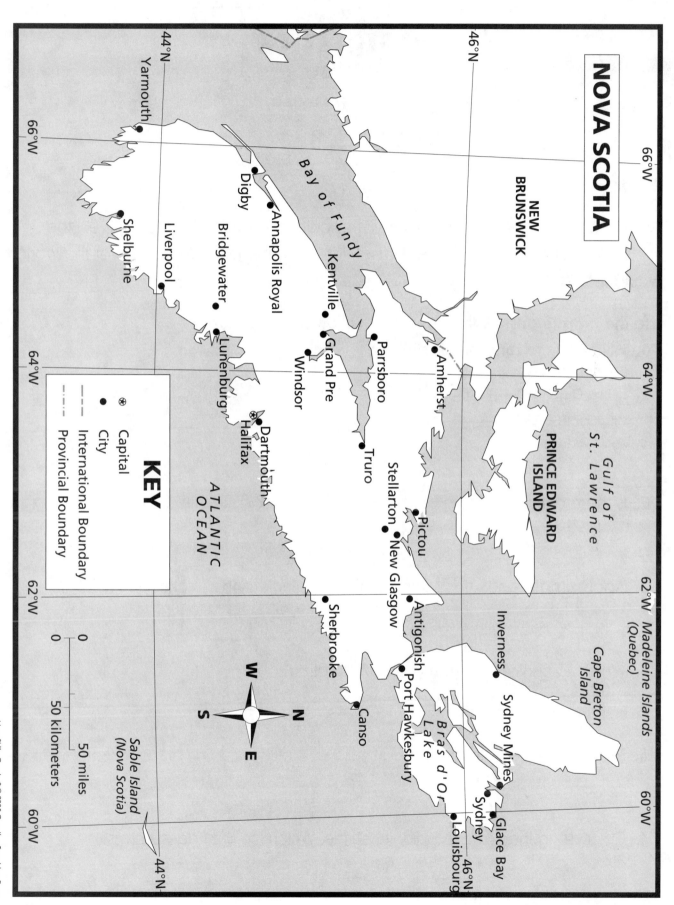

NOVA SCOTIA

NEW BRUNSWICK

PRINCE EDWARD ISLAND

Gulf of St. Lawrence

Madeleine Islands (Quebec)

Cape Breton Island

Bay of Fundy

Yarmouth

Shelburne

Digby

Liverpool

Bridgewater

Annapolis Royal

Lunenburg

Kentville

Grand Pre

Windsor

Parsboro

Amherst

⊛ Halifax
Dartmouth

ATLANTIC OCEAN

Truro

Stellarton

New Glasgow

Pictou

Sherbrooke

Antigonish

Port Hawkesbury

Canso

Inverness

Bras d'Or Lake

Sydney Mines

Sydney

Glace Bay

Louisbourg

Sable Island (Nova Scotia)

KEY

⊛ Capital
● City
- - - International Boundary
 ...... Provincial Boundary

N
W   E
S

0   50 kilometers
0   50 miles

44°N

46°N

66°W

64°W

62°W

60°W

Map Skills: Grade 3 © 2005 Creative Teaching Press

Name_____ **Date**_____

Antarctica
Review

Read.

Antarctica is a continent of extremes: the coldest recorded temperatures, the windiest coasts, the thickest ice. In fact, if the ice melted, the oceans of the world would rise 200 feet (60 m)!

Use the map to answer the questions. Follow the directions.
You will need crayons for this activity.

1. Draw a red star on the South Pole. Find the South Magnetic Pole and circle it in brown.

2. Is there a compass rose on this map? Why not?

   _____

3. Approximately how far is it from Mt. Kirkpatrick to the thickest ice?

   _____

4. Which 2 countries claim land near Antarctica?

   _____   _____

5. Draw along the Antarctic Circle in yellow.

6. Color along the prime meridian in purple. Which ice shelf does it cross?

   _____

Map Skills: Grade 3 © 2005 Creative Teaching Press

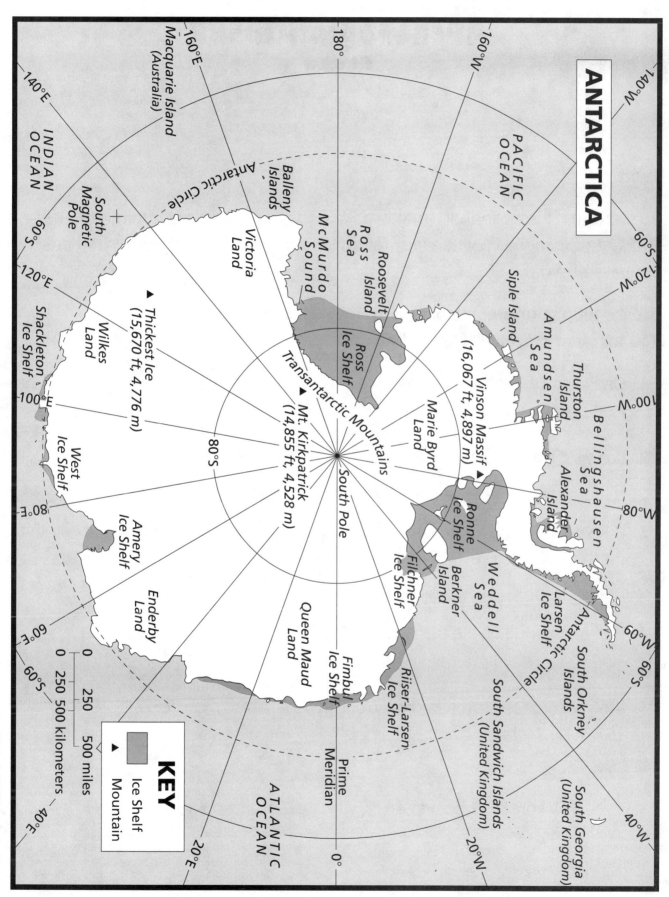

ANTARCTICA

PACIFIC OCEAN

140°W

160°W

180°

160°E

Macquarie Island (Australia)

140°E

INDIAN OCEAN

120°E

100°E

80°E

60°E

40°E

20°E

0°

Prime Meridian

20°W

40°W

60°W

80°W

100°W

120°W

Antarctic Circle

60°S

60°S

60°S

80°S

South Pole

Balleny Islands

McMurdo Sound

Ross Sea

Roosevelt Island

Ross Ice Shelf

Siple Island

Amundsen Sea

Thurston Island

Bellingshausen Sea

Alexander Island

South Orkney Islands (United Kingdom)

South Sandwich Islands (United Kingdom)

South Georgia (United Kingdom)

Marie Byrd Land

Vinson Massif (16,067 ft, 4,897 m) ▲

Larsen Ice Shelf

Antarctic Circle

Ronne Ice Shelf

▲

Berkner Island

Weddell Sea

Filchner Ice Shelf

Riiser-Larsen Ice Shelf

Fimbul Ice Shelf

Queen Maud Land

Enderby Land

Amery Ice Shelf

West Ice Shelf

Shackleton Ice Shelf

Wilkes Land

South Magnetic Pole

+

Victoria Land

Transantarctic Mountains

▲ Mt. Kikpatrick (14,855 ft, 4,528 m)

▲ Thickest Ice (15,670 ft, 4,776 m)

ATLANTIC OCEAN

KEY

Ice Shelf

▲ Mountain

0 250 500 kilometers

0 250 500 miles

Map Skills: Grade 3 © 2005 Creative Teaching Press

Name_____ Date_____

Anchorage, Alaska
Review

Read.

Anchorage is the largest city in Alaska. Wild salmon travel right through the city in Ship Creek Salmon Run when they return from the ocean to the stream where they were born.

Use the map to answer the questions. Follow the directions.
You will need crayons for this activity.

1. On this map, what island is farthest southwest? _____

2. Use your ruler. Which is farther from Kodiak: Seward or Lime Village?

   _____

3. Use your blue crayon to circle the key. Could you find the capital city on this map? (The key gives you a hint.) _____

4. Find Anchorage on the map and circle it in red.

5. Use your orange crayon to draw along 150°W. Which mountain is closer to 150°W: Mt. McKinley or Mt. Veniaminof? _____

6. If you flew from Dillingham to Aniak, which direction would you travel?

   _____

Map Skills: Grade 3 © 2005 Creative Teaching Press

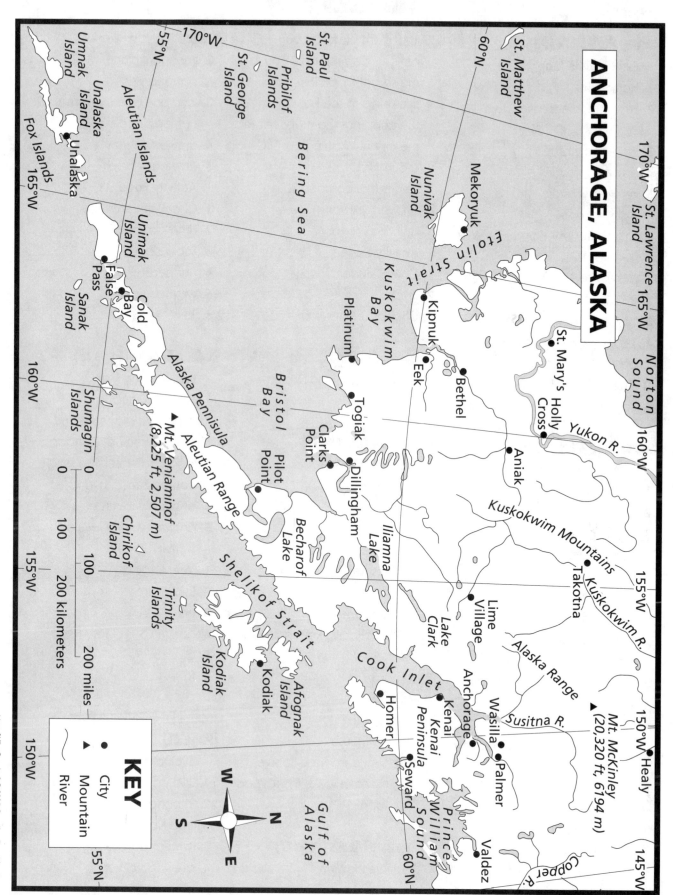

ANCHORAGE, ALASKA

KEY

● City
▲ Mountain
〜 River

N
W E
S

170°W
165°W
160°W
155°W
150°W
145°W

60°N
55°N

Norton Sound

St. Lawrence Island

St. Matthew Island

Etolin Strait

Mekoryuk

Nunivak Island

Bering Sea

St. Paul Island

Pribilof Islands

St. George Island

Aleutian Islands

Unalaska Island
Umnak Island

Fox Islands

Unalaska

Unimak Island

False Pass
Cold Bay

Sanak Island

Shumagin Islands

Alaska Peninsula

Chirikof Island

▲ Mt. Veniaminof
(8,225 ft, 2,507 m)

Aleutian Range

Trinity Islands

Shelikof Strait

Kodiak Island

Kodiak

Afognak Island

Becharof Lake

Pilot Point

Bristol Bay

Clarks Point

Dillingham

Togiak

Platinum

Kuskokwim Bay

Kipnuk
Eek

Bethel

St. Mary's
Holly Cross

Yukon R.

Aniak

Kuskokwim Mountains

Iliamna Lake

Lake Clark

Lime Village

Takotna

Kuskokwim R.

Mt. McKinley
(20,320 ft, 6194 m) ▲

Healy

Alaska Range

Susitna R.

Wasilla
Palmer

Anchorage

Kenai Peninsula

Kenai

Cook Inlet

Homer

Seward

Prince William Sound

Valdez

Copper R.

Gulf of Alaska

0   100   100   200 kilometers
0   100   100   200 miles

Map Skills: Grade 3 © 2005 Creative Teaching Press

Answer Key

Hockey Puck Park (Page 9)

Evaluate the Map
1. Hockey Puck Park
2. key places in Hockey Puck Park
3. land and water
4. answers will vary
5. answers will vary

Activity Page
1. Check student work to be sure the activity is possible in the park.
2. 2
3. yes
4. Yes, because there is a parking lot there.
5. Check student work.
6. Edge Lane and Bruiser Avenue

Map of Olde Albion (Page 11)

Evaluate the Map
1. Map of Olde Albion
2. key places in Olde Albion
3. land and water, key
4. answers will vary
5. answers will vary

Activity Page
1. Check student work. There are 5 games symbols.
2. food
3. Check student work. It is near Renaissance Lake.
4. yes
5. Check student work. It should follow Houndsman Lane.
6. Olde Globe Theater

The Capitol (Page 13)

Evaluate the Map
1. The Capitol
2. important places in our nation's capital (Note:You may want to explain that the title refers to the building in the center of the map, not to the city of Washington, D.C. around it.)
3. key, scale, compass rose
4. answers will vary
5. answers will vary

Activity Page
1. Check student work.
2. I395
3. Check student work.
4. E. Capitol St.
5. the Longworth Building
6. Russell Building and Dirksen Building

San Antonio, TX (Page 15)

Evaluate the Map
1. San Antonio, Texas
2. important places in San Antonio, Texas
3. key, scale, compass rose
4. answers will vary
5. answers will vary

Activity Page
1. Southern Pacific Railroad
2. the theater
3. Lamar St.
4. No. Booker Alley does not go to the library.
5. the courthouse
6. Check student work. Be sure they do not mistake the railroad for a road.

The San Juan Islands (Page 17)

Evaluate the Map
1. The San Juan Islands
2. important places of the San Juan Islands
3. land and water, key, scale, compass rose
4. answers will vary
5. answers will vary

Activity Page
1. Check student work.
2. Lime Kiln Point State Park
3. Sucia Island
4. northeast
5. west
6. 15

Regina, Canada (Page 19)

Evaluate the Map
1. Regina, Canada
2. important places in and around Regina, Canada
3. land and water, key, scale, compass rose, grid lines
4. answers will vary
5. answers will vary

Activity Page
1. true; Regina
2. Esk, Watrous, Simpson, Craik
3. east
4. column 5
5. C
6. false

Joshua Tree National Park (Page 21)

Evaluate the Map
1. Joshua Tree National Park
2. important places in Joshua Tree National Park
3. land and water, key
4. answers will vary

5. answers will vary
   Activity Page
1. yes
2. no
3. Belle
4. Check student work.
5. Check student work. There is only one medical facility.
6. no

Horsethief Canyon (Page 23)
   Evaluate the Map
1. Horsethief Canyon
2. important places in the neighborhood of Horsethief Canyon
3. key, scale, compass rose, grid lines
4. answers will vary
5. answers will vary
   Activity Page
1. Check student work; longer
2. Gold Rush Dr.
3. 1 1/8" —okay to accept 1", 38 mm—okay to accept 4 cm; more than
4. Check student work.
5. D3, D4, C4, C5
6. Check student work.

Petaluma, CA (Page 25)
   Evaluate the Map
1. Petaluma, CA
2. important places in Petaluma, CA
3. key, scale, compass rose, grid lines
4. answers will vary
5. answers will vary
   Activity Page
1. McDowell Park
2. Check student work; B1, C1, D1

3. Check student work.
4. Check student work; B3, B4
5. the pool
6. Check student work.

Pirate Map (Page 27)
   Evaluate the Map
1. Pirate Map
2. key places used to find the buried treasure
3. land and water, scale
4. answers will vary
5. answers will vary
   Activity Page
1. 28 1/3"
2. Check student work.
3. 10 mi
4. Black Lagoon
5. ~20 mi
6. ~5 mi

Japan 1 (Page 29)
   Evaluate the Map
1. Japan
2. important places in Japan
3. land and water, key, scale, compass rose, latitude, longitude
4. answers will vary
5. answers will vary
   Activity Page
1. Check student work; Tokyo
2. Japan, Russia, China, North Korea, South Korea
3. northwest
4. Check student work. Be sure that students do not include the border between China and North Korea.
5. no
6. Check student work.

Japan 2 (Page 31)
   Evaluate the Map
1. Japan
2. important physical features of Japan
3. land and water, key, scale, compass rose
4. answers will vary
5. answers will vary
   Activity Page
1. Check student work. Be sure that students color the river in South Korea and the lake in Russia colored.
2. Sea of Japan (also called East Sea), Korea Strait, East China Sea, Philippine Sea, Pacific Ocean, Sea of Oshotsk
3. no
4. 3
5. Check student work; 1
6. southwest

South America (Page 33)
   Evaluate the Map
1. South America
2. important places in South America
3. land and water, key, scale, compass rose, latitude, longitude
4. answers will vary
5. answers will vary
   Activity Page
1. Check student work.
2. $10°N$
3. $20°S$
4. north
5. Ecuador, Colombia, Brazil
6. 4

Asia (Page 35)
Evaluate the Map
1. Asia
2. important places in Asia
3. land and water, key, scale, compass rose, latitude, longitude
4. answers will vary
5. answers will vary
Activity Page
1. Check student work.
2. Check student work.
3. true
4. 50°E
5. 80°E
6. Check student work. (40°E)

Fargo, North Dakota (Page 37)
Evaluate the Map
1. Fargo, North Dakota
2. important places in Fargo, ND
3. land and water, key, scale, compass rose, grid lines
4. answers will vary
5. answers will vary
Activity Page
1. 1st Ave. N., Highway 10, Center Ave.
2. C3
3. Woodlawn Park
4. No; according to the key, the arrow indicates this is a one-way street going north
5. no
6. Check student work. The correct location is in D2.

Idaho Falls, Idaho (Page 39)
Evaluate the Map
1. Idaho Falls, Idaho
2. important places in Idaho Falls, ID
3. land and water, key, scale,

compass rose, grid lines
4. answers will vary
5. answers will vary
Activity Page
1. Check student work.
2. west
3. north on S. Colorado Ave., west in Highway 20, north on Saturn Ave., west on Casseopeia St.
4. ├──┼──┼──┤
5. Vassar Way C1

Nova Scotia (Page 41)
Evaluate the Map
1. Nova Scotia
2. important places in Nova Scotia
3. land and water, key, scale, compass rose
4. answers will vary
5. answers will vary
Activity Page
1. Check student work. Be sure students do not include the international boundary.
2. Check student work; Yes
3. no
4. northeast
5. ~360 mi, ~580 km
6. Shelburne

Antarctica (Page 43)
Evaluate the Map
1. Antarctica
2. important places on the continent of Antarctica
3. land and water, key, scale, latitude, longitude
4. answers will vary
5. answers will vary

Activity Page
1. Check student work.
2. No; Possibale answer:the center of the map is the farthest point south. North is the direction away from the center of the map.
3. 1000 mi, 1610 km (note:the scale on this map is extremely small and greater variation in answers may be expected.)
4. United Kingdom and Australia
5. Check student work.
6. Check student work; Fimbul Ice Shelf

Anchorage, Alaska (Page 45)
Evaluate the Map
1. Anchorage, Alaska
2. important places in Alaska
3. land and water, key, scale, compass rose, latitude, longitude
4. answers will vary
5. answers will vary
Activity Page
1. Umnak Island
2. Lime Village
3. Check student work; no.
4. Check student work.
5. Check student work; Mt. McKinley.
6. north